21st Century Skills Library

REAL WORLD SCIENCE

EARTH'S BIOMES

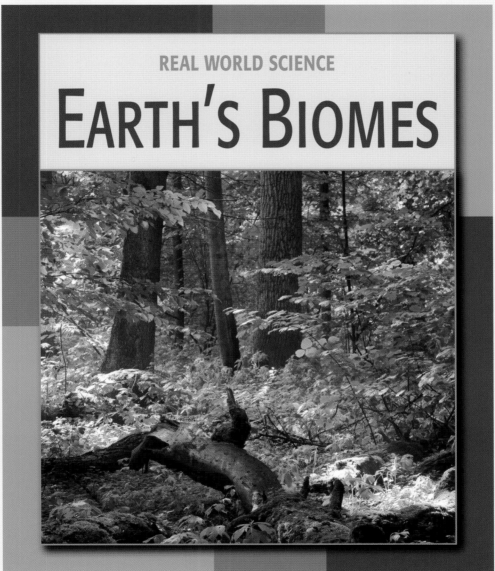

Katy S. Duffield

Cherry Lake Publishing
Ann Arbor, Michigan

CHERRY
LAKE
Publishing

Published in the United States of America by Cherry Lake Publishing
Ann Arbor, Michigan
www.cherrylakepublishing.com

Content Adviser: Laura Graceffa, middle school science teacher; BA degree in science, Vassar College; MA degrees in science and education, Brown University

Photo Credits: Cover and page 1, © Aleksander Bolbot/Shutterstock; page 4, © Lee Prince/Shutterstock; page 7, © Christophe Robard/Shutterstock; page 8, © Boleslaw Kubica/Shutterstock; page 10, © Robert Shantz/Alamy; page 11, © Pakhnyushcha/Shutterstock; page 14, © Ralph Loesche/Shutterstock; page 16, © STILLFX/Shutterstock; page 18, © Nymph/Shutterstock; page 20, © Wolfgang Zintl/Shutterstock; page 21, Fletcher & Baylis/Photo Researchers, Inc.; page 23, © Naturablitcher/Shutterstock; page 24, © Alan Scheer/Shutterstock; page 26, © Bob Gibbons/Alamy; page 27, © Willem Timms/Shutterstock

Library of Congress Cataloging-in-Publication Data

Duffield, Katy.
Earth's biomes / by Katy S. Duffield.
   p. cm.—(Real world science)
ISBN-13: 978-1-60279-457-3
ISBN-10: 1-60279-457-X
1. Biotic communities—Juvenile literature. I. Title. II. Series.

QH541.14.D84 2009
577—dc22   2008040803

Cherry Lake Publishing would like to acknowledge the work of
The Partnership for 21st Century Skills.
Please visit www.21stcenturyskills.org for more information.

TABLE OF CONTENTS

CHAPTER ONE

EARTH'S DRIEST BIOME

Earth's biomes support all different types of plants and animals.

Our Earth is an amazing place. As far as we know, there is no other place quite like it in the universe. Plants and animals of all kinds can be found throughout the world. But different plants and animals are suited to different environments.

Scientists have a special name for these different environments, which may be far apart but have the same **climate** and the same kinds of plants and animals. They call these groups of places biomes. Deserts, deciduous forests, tropical rain forests, taiga, arctic tundra, and grasslands are the world's six major biomes.

Many factors affect how biomes form. One is precipitation. Forests grow in places that get a lot of rain. Temperature is another factor. It affects the type of forest that grows. Rain forests grow in hot climates. Deciduous forests grow in colder climates.

Earth's driest biome is the desert. Deserts cover about one-fifth of the Earth's land surface. Many people think of deserts as places where there is no water. But even the driest places on Earth get *some* rain, dew, or other forms of precipitation. Scientists define a desert by looking at *how much* precipitation an area gets. Places that get less than 10 inches (25.4 cm) of precipitation each year are considered deserts.

REAL WORLD SCIENCE CHALLENGE

A **climograph** is a chart of an area's weather. It shows average temperatures and precipitation. To make a climograph, visit www.weatherbase.com or www.worldclimate.com. Type the name of your city, then click on the link for average rainfall. To make a chart, write the name of your city and "Average Rainfall" at the top of a sheet of paper. Then list the names of the months in a row from left to right. Use the Web site to find the average rainfall for each month. Enter the figures on your chart. Based on your chart, do you think you live in a desert? Why or why not? (You can also do this for another city and then compare the results of both.)

(Turn to page 29 for the answer)

Most people also think of deserts as places of scorching sun and constant extreme heat. Deserts are indeed the hottest places in the world. The Sahara in North Africa is a huge, hot desert. Daytime summer temperatures in the Sahara have reached 136°F (57.7°C). But the nights and winters in the Sahara are much cooler. In the winter, temperatures can fall below freezing (32°F or 0°C).

There are hot deserts like the Sahara, but there are cold deserts, too.

These cold deserts get their small amount of water in the form of snow

or fog. They can be found in China, Russia, the United States, and other

places in Asia, South America, and Africa. Not many people think of

ice-covered Antarctica as a desert. But it is. The temperature there

hardly ever rises above freezing, and has dropped to -128.6° F (-89.2° C).

The sun beats down on sand dunes in Africa's huge Sahara Desert.

The barrel cactus (pictured) stores water to survive in the hot, dry desert.

Antarctica's snowfall is only equal to around 2 inches (5 cm) of precipitation each year. That makes it a desert.

Life in the desert can be harsh. Plants and animals must adapt to very dry conditions. They must also adapt to extreme temperatures. Desert plants and animals have special features that help them survive.

Most desert plants are succulents. Succulents store water in their stems, roots, or leaves. This helps them survive long dry periods. Most succulents, such as cactus, have fleshy parts with a waxy surface that holds in water. Other desert plants have very long roots that reach water sources deep underground.

Animals have to adapt to survive in the desert, too. In hot deserts, prairie dogs and snakes find ways to stay cool. They dig burrows. They stay underground during the heat of the day. Kangaroo rats have no sweat glands. Their bodies lose almost no water. They get all the water they need from the

For this activity, get in touch with your creative side. Think about and design an imaginary plant or animal that might live in the desert. Draw a picture of the plant or animal. Write a paragraph or two describing how that plant or animal might survive in the desert. Be sure to show and describe the special features that allow it to adapt to harsh desert conditions. Show how it copes with the desert heat or cold. Show how it gets the water it needs to survive.

A kangaroo rat searches for seeds, which provide both food and water.

seeds they eat. This means they never have to drink. Other desert creatures

nibble on succulents to get their water. Large desert animals such as camels

can go for weeks without water. Their tough feet aren't burned by hot

sands and their coat reflects sunlight. As in all biomes, plants and animals

of the desert do what they have to in order to survive.

CHAPTER TWO

TWO KINDS OF FORESTS

Cool, shady deciduous forests are another of Earth's biomes.

Two of Earth's major biomes are forests. Forests are large areas covered by lots of trees. They are found all over the world except where the climate is always very cold or very dry. But not all forests are alike.

One type of forest is the deciduous forest. Deciduous forests are found across North America, Asia, and Europe. They have hot summers and cold winters. Each year 30 to 60 inches (75–150 cm) of precipitation fall there. Deciduous forests also have four seasons. The seasons are important to the plants that live there.

Maples, elms, and oaks are deciduous trees. These trees have broad leaves. If the trees kept their leaves during cold winters, they could not survive. The water in the leaves would freeze and damage the trees. To keep that from happening, changes take place during autumn. The trees begin to sense the changes of shorter days and colder temperatures. Leaf color changes from green to red, gold, and orange. When winter arrives, leaves turn brown and fall from the trees.

REAL WORLD SCIENCE CHALLENGE

To learn more about about deciduous trees, visit a nearby forest or park. Do you see any deciduous trees? If so, what evidence tells you they are deciduous? Observe the leaves of the trees. How might you determine the season just by looking at the leaves? If possible, collect leaves from different trees to identify later.

(Turn to page 29 for the answer)

Animals too must adapt to the seasons. Winters can be quite cold. Many birds migrate, or fly to warmer areas, until spring. Black bears survive the cold in another way. They spend winters hibernating, or in a deep sleep, in their dens. Food can also be scarce in the winter. Squirrels gather and store nuts to help them survive.

Another forest biome is the tropical rain forest. Tropical rain forests are found near the equator. The climate is hot and wet all year. Rain forests get

The rain forest canopy provides homes for many animals.

from 80 to 400 inches (200–1,000 cm) of rainfall each year. That is as much as

33 feet (10 m) of rainfall in a single year! No other biome receives more rain.

Rain forests cover only about 6 percent of the Earth's land surface.

Yet more than half of the world's plant and animal species live there.

The warm, wet weather helps plants thrive. With lots of food, water, and

shelter, animals thrive in the rain forest, too.

The rain forest is made up of four main layers. In the top layer, giant trees tower high above all the others. These trees are called emergents. The tallest trees can grow to heights of 200 feet (60 m). Butterflies, monkeys, and eagles are at home here.

The second layer lies below the emergents. It is called the canopy. Trees in the canopy grow from 60 to 100 feet (18 to 30 m). Most of the animal species in the rain forest live in the canopy. Toucans, sloths, and lizards fly, leap, and climb from tree to tree in the canopy.

21st Century Content

The world's rain forests are shrinking. Over the years, millions of acres of rain forest trees have been cut down. People use wood from the trees for home building, furniture, and firewood. They cut down trees to make roads. Or they use the cleared land for farming or cattle grazing. When land is cleared, animals like jaguars and anteaters are forced to find new homes. Pollution poisons bodies of water and kills the fish that live there. Plants and trees that are destroyed may never grow back.

The rain forest isn't the only biome whose plants and animals are threatened. Tree clearing, road building, farming, and pollution take their toll in all the major biomes. Steps are being taken to help control the destruction but there is still much work to be done.

Below the canopy is the **understory**. The canopy blocks some of the

sunlight from the understory. With less sunlight, plants grow more slowly.

Small trees and shrubs are the main plants of the understory. Lots of

insects and animals such as jaguars and leopards are found there.

Animals small and large share a home in the rain forest understory.

The bottom layer of the rain forest is the forest floor. Not much sunlight reaches the forest floor. Without sunlight, few large plants grow. But bacteria and fungi thrive. Gorillas, anteaters, insects, and spiders all live on the forest floor.

Forests are an important part of our world. They provide food and shelter for many millions of animal and plant species. And the trees help keep our air healthy and clean.

Each year Janalee Caldwell spends four months in the Amazon rain forest of South America. Janalee is an ecologist. Ecologists are scientists who study plants and animals and the way they interact in their environment. They want to learn more about the way the world works. Janalee studies poisonous frogs and tadpoles. She watches how the frogs live and what they eat. Janalee has spent hours in the pouring rain to watch the frogs. She says, "If you want to know what's happening, you've got to be out there." Janalee's research helps us learn how the rain forest works. It also teaches us about connections between rain forest plants and animals.

CHAPTER THREE

FRIGID WINTER BIOMES

Winter in the taiga is cold and snowy and just right for the growth of evergreen trees.

The taiga is the world's largest land biome. It covers parts of North America, Asia, and Europe. The taiga lies north of the deciduous forests.

Summer temperatures in the taiga can reach around 75° F (23.8° C). Winters are very cold and snowy. Winter temperatures can fall to -65° F (-53.9° C).

Fifteen to 30 inches (38–76 cm) of rain and snow fall in the taiga each year.

The taiga is made up mostly of coniferous trees. Coniferous

trees are evergreens. They have needles instead of leaves. They

have cones rather than flowers. Spruce, pine, and fir are coniferous

trees. These trees adapt well to the taiga's climate. Since they

are cone-shaped, snow slides easily off their branches. If heavy

snows could not slide off, the weight of the snow might break the

trees' limbs.

REAL WORLD SCIENCE CHALLENGE

Roll a sheet of green construction paper into a cone shape. Tape the edges so it holds its shape. Stand the cone upright on a paper plate. You may need to trim the bottom of the cone to get it to stand. Imagine the cone is an evergreen tree. Ask permission to use a small amount of table salt. (If you don't have salt, sand will also work.) The salt represents snow. Slowly sprinkle a small amount of salt onto the cone. What happens when the "snow" hits the "evergreen"? Why is this a good thing for the evergreen?

(Turn to page 29 for the answer)

The lynx's heavy fur coat and large paws allow it to survive in the taiga.

Many animals also live in the taiga. To survive, they must prepare for the cold winters. Grizzly bears, for instance, hunt for food all summer. They eat as much as they can and put on a thick layer of fat. The fat helps them stay warm. So do the caves where they rest until the weather warms. Other animals, like the Canada lynx, grow thick coats to protect them from the cold. Lots of insects can be found in the taiga, too. Moths, flies, and mosquitoes thrive there during the warm months. Birds, like finches and sparrows, arrive in the spring. They feast on the insects that swarm there.

The taiga has very cold winters. But it is not the coldest biome. The arctic tundra holds that record. The arctic tundra is north of the taiga, near the North Pole. Only about fifty-five days of the year have temperatures above freezing. Even in the summer, temperatures rise only to around 50° F (10° C). The arctic tundra is also very dry. It usually gets less than 10 inches (25.4 cm) of rain or snow each year. In many ways, it could be considered a cold desert. There is one difference though. Unlike the desert, the arctic tundra sometimes has areas of standing water in the summer.

Moss and lichen grow on rocks during the short summer in the arctic tundra.

REAL WORLD SCIENCE CHALLENGE

Scientists believe that the Earth's climate is changing. They believe the Earth is getting warmer. They think this is happening because large amounts of carbon dioxide and other gases are trapping heat in the atmosphere. Some think that as temperatures rise, much of the ice in the arctic tundra and other areas could begin to melt. How might rising temperatures and melting ice affect the kinds of plants and animals that can survive in the tundra?

(Turn to page 29 for the answer)

The ground in the arctic tundra stays frozen most of the year. A layer of frozen soil sits just below the ground's surface. This soil is called **permafrost**. During the summer, the arctic tundra gets almost twenty-four hours of sunlight each day. This sunlight allows some of the soil above the permafrost to thaw. The growing season is too short for trees. Shrubs and grasses grow in the thawed soil. Mosses, lichens, and other small plants grow on rocks on the ground. Animals such as caribou and musk oxen feed on these plants.

Almost no reptiles or amphibians can live in the tundra. Only about forty-eight species of land mammals make their homes there. Musk

Heavily furred musk oxen are one of the few species that can survive in the tundra.

oxen have a thick, layered coat of fur to keep them warm. The Arctic fox's footpads are covered with thick fur. This helps the fox travel on ice and in deep snow. Caribou and some birds spend only the summers in the tundra. In the winter, they migrate to other areas.

Conditions in the taiga and tundra are harsh. It takes special kinds of plants and animals to survive there.

CHAPTER FOUR

GRASS AS FAR AS THE EYE CAN SEE

A cottontail rabbit hides in prairie grass, a common feature of the grasslands biome.

It is easy to guess the main plant type in a grasslands biome—grass! Grasslands can be found on every continent except Antarctica. They are mainly located between forests and deserts. Most grasslands are large and flat and nearly treeless. Grasslands get between 19 and 35 inches of precipitation (50–90 cm) each year.

Rainfall plays a big role in grasslands. If grasslands were wetter, trees would grow and they would be forests. If grasslands were drier, very little would grow and they would be deserts. The only trees that can be found in grasslands grow near a water source such as a river or lake.

REAL WORLD SCIENCE CHALLENGE

Think about the conditions different plants need to survive. Do you think a cactus could thrive in the tundra? Why or why not? Do you think a rain forest plant could live in the desert? Why or why not? Could a maple tree grow successfully on the rain forest floor? Why or why not?

(Turn to page 29 for the answer)

There are two main kinds of grasslands. One is temperate. Temperate grasslands have hot summers and cold winters. The prairies of the Great Plains in North America are examples of temperate grasslands. These prairies get a fair amount of rain. This allows grasses to grow two to five feet (61–152 cm) tall.

Another example of a temperate grassland is a **steppe**. A steppe is usually drier than a prairie. With less rain, grass in the steppe grows shorter than in the prairie. This grass is usually less than 2 feet (61 cm) tall.

Temperate grasslands are home to lots of animals and insects. There is plenty of food and shelter for them there. Skunks, raccoons, and rabbits skitter through the prairie grass. Large grazing animals like bison and antelope are also suited to grasslands. Grasshoppers hop and snakes slither. Butterflies and hawks soar overhead.

Temperate grassland provides good grazing land for horses, antelope, and bison.

The other kind of grassland is tropical. Tropical grasslands are called **savannas**. Savannas cover nearly half of Africa. Their

The savanna's tall grass and low trees supply food for giraffes and other creatures.

climate is warm or hot. They have both rainy and

dry seasons. Most savanna rainfall comes in the

summer months. Winters are usually dry. Like all

grasslands, savannas are mostly grass. But savannas

have some trees. Acacia and baobab trees grow alone

or in small groups on the savanna.

The savanna is also home to many animals. Impalas

and wildebeests roam the grasslands to find food. They

graze on the grasses that grow there. Giraffes stretch their long necks to the

top of the acacia trees to nibble their leaves. Lions and leopards come to the

grassland for food, too. But they don't graze. They come to hunt the grazing

animals. Water buffalo, zebras, and ostriches make their homes there, too.

REAL WORLD SCIENCE CHALLENGE

Consider all the biomes you have read about. Without looking back in the book, can you remember which biome gets the most precipitation? The least? List the biomes in order, starting with the biome that you think gets the most rain/snow each year and ending with the one that gets the least. Then look back at the book, if needed. Make a bar graph showing each of the six biomes and their average yearly precipitation. Compare the bar graph to your list. Did you remember the biome with the highest precipitation? The lowest? What factors helped you remember?

(Turn to page 29 for the answer)

Desert. Deciduous forest. Tropical rain forest. Taiga. Tundra.

Grasslands. The biomes of the Earth are all unique. Each biome has an

important role in our amazing world.

REAL WORLD SCIENCE CHALLENGE ANSWERS

Chapter One
Page 6

Add together the rainfall totals for all the months on your chart. Look at the final number. Deserts get less than 10 inches (25.4 cm) of rain each year. Is your number less than 10? If so, you live in a desert biome. If it's more than 10, you do not live in a desert.

Chapter Two
Page 13

Did you see trees with broad leaves? Brown leaves on the ground? Leaves changing color? All these are signs of deciduous trees. Green leaves are usually found in spring and/or summer. If the leaves are red, gold, or orange, it may be autumn. Brown leaves on the ground are signs of winter.

Chapter Three
Page 19

The tree's cone shape helps the snow slide off. If snow piled up instead of sliding off, branches could break off and damage the tree.

Page 22

Animals used to living in cold, snow, and ice may have to leave the area. Or they may have to find ways to adapt to the changing climate. Mosses and lichens that some animals eat may be taken over. Taller plants and shrubs that thrive in warmer, wetter areas may take their place.

Chapter Four
Page 25

A cactus could not live in the arctic tundra. Cacti cannot live in very cold temperatures. Rain forest plants would not survive in the dry desert. They are not adapted to hold in water like cacti. Maples need sunlight to grow and thrive. The rain forest floor gets little sunlight, so it would be hard for maples to grow there.

Page 28

1. Rain forest   80–400 inches (200–1,000 cm)
2. Deciduous forest   30–60 inches (75–150 cm)
3. Grasslands   19–35 inches (50–90 cm)
4. Taiga   15–30 inches (38–76 cm)
5. Tundra   less than 10 inches (25.4 cm)
6. Desert   less than 10 inches (25.4 cm)

GLOSSARY

adapt (uh-DAPT) to change or adjust in some way that makes a plant or animal more successful in a particular environment

biome (BY-ohm) a large region with a distinct climate and a distinct community of plants and animals that exist there

canopy (KAN-uh-pee) the densest layer of a forest, taller than all other layers except emergent trees

climate (KLY-mit) the weather conditions, such as average temperature and rainfall, of a particular area

climograph (KLY-mo-graf) a graph or chart that shows the climate of a particular area, including such information as average temperature and rainfall

coniferous (koh-NIF-er-us) trees, usually evergreens, that bear cones

deciduous (di-SID-yoo-us) trees that lose their leaves at the end of the growing season

permafrost (PURR-muh-frawst) a layer of permanently frozen ground

precipitation (pre-sip-i-TAY-shun) water released from clouds in the form of rain, freezing rain, sleet, snow, or hail

savanna (suh-VAN-uh) flat grassland found in hot, dry regions

steppe (STEP) flat, grass-covered plains that receive low rainfall

temperate (TEM-per-it) areas with moderate temperatures, neither very hot nor very cold

understory (UN-dur-stor-ee) the underlying layer of vegetation, especially the plants that grow beneath a forest's canopy

FOR MORE INFORMATION

Books and DVDs

Davis, Barbara J. *Biomes and Ecosystems*. Chicago: Gareth Stevens, 2007.

Kirchner, Renee. *Biomes*. Farmington Hills, MI: KidHaven, 2006.

Way Cool Science: Biotrackers—Biomes and Habitats. DVD. Mazzarella Media, 2007.

Web Sites

Biomes of the World
www.thewildclassroom.com/biomes/
Learn more about biomes on this interesting site. And don't miss the "Scientist Profiles." The profiles are packed with information about the work of biome scientists.

Center for Educational Technologies—Biomes
www.cotf.edu/ete/modules/msese/earthsysflr/biomes.html
This site has information about the plants and animals of each biome. It also tells more about climographs.

Missouri Botanical Gardens—What's It Like Where You Live?
www.mbgnet.net/index.html
This site is packed with facts and photos of the various biomes.

NASA—Mission: Biomes
http://earthobservatory.nasa.gov/Laboratory/Biome
This NASA Web site contains biome maps and descriptions and links to other biome sites.

INDEX

ABOUT THE AUTHOR

Katy S. Duffield has been writing for children and young adults for over ten years. She has written books on topics such as poltergeists, the Bermuda Triangle, the developers of YouTube and PlayStation, and several others. Katy also writes picture books for younger readers and has written for many children's magazines.